MW00700927

Coloring Books for Kids & Toddlers:
Animals Coloring

by Jane J. R.

Coloring Books for Kids & Toddlers: Animals Coloring by Jane J. R.

Sea Animals, Farm Animals, Jungle Animals, Woodland Animals and Circus Animals

The pages of this book are suitable for crayons and colored pencils for kids.
Each picture is printed on one side of 60 lb pure white paper to minimize scoring and bleed-through. It is also suitable for framing. Parents should teach children how to use this book and media properly.

The age when a child is ready to begin using coloring books varies from child to child.

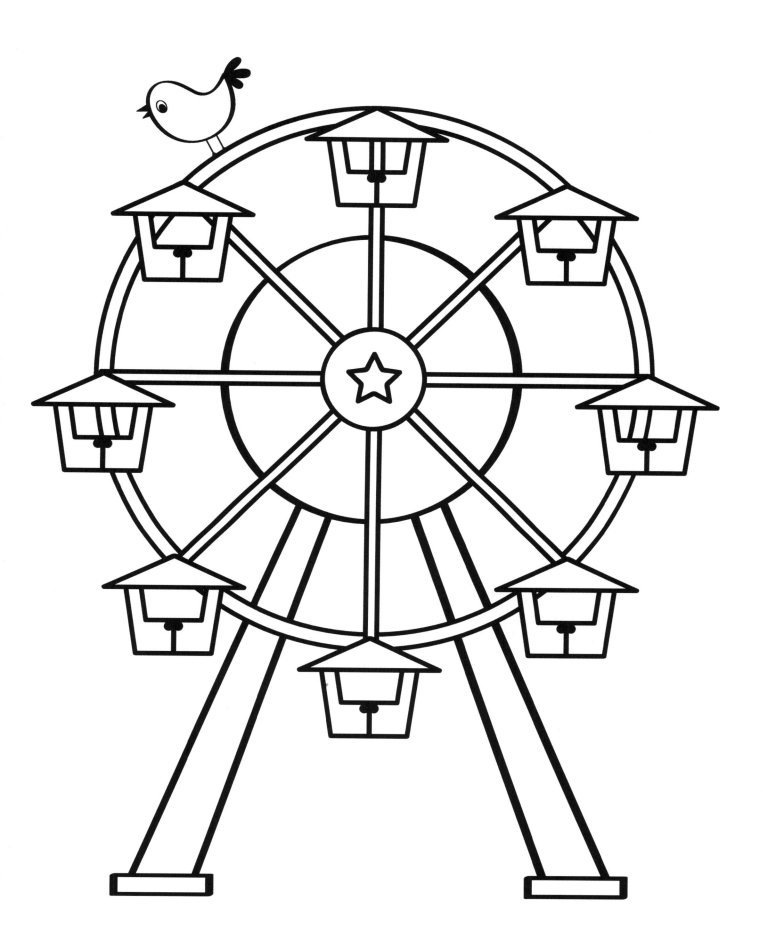

Made in the USA
San Bernardino, CA
15 October 2017